LAUGHING WITH THE BEAR

LAUGHING WITH THE BEAR

THE BEAR

Humorous Tales of a Coaching Legend

Roll Tide

RICHARD SIKES

Richard Ske

Old Bay Publishing
Madison, Alabama

Library of Congress Cataloging-in-Publication data is available.
ISBN: 0-9745854-0-8

Cover design by Hope Design
Page design by Mike Towle

Printed in the United States of America
1 2 3 4 5 6 — 07 06 05 04 03

To Nell and Matthew

Contents

IV. Home at the Capstone

Foreword

I T'S BEEN ABOUT A quarter of a century since I
played football for Coach Bryant at the University
of Alabama. Yet my memories of him are as vivid now
as they were right after I took my last snap from center as a member of the Crimson Tide. I can still see
the houndstooth hat gracing the Saturday afternoon
sideline, and I believe I can still hear the low, grizzled
speech of Coach Bryant inspiring us in the locker
room before a game or during halftime.

There is no easy way to put into words the pro-
found effect Coach Bryant had on me, both profes-
sionally and personally. He was an intense competitor, to be sure, and second to none when it came to
inspiring players and devising game strategy. Yet I
can't recall his ever losing his cool, waving his arms
around, or berating someone just for effect. He knew
how to win, and in that regard he had a distinguished confidence that carried over into all of his
actions and his words. One thing I know for sure—
when I was nearly killed recently in a traffic acci-
dent, a large part of my inspiration to recovery was

remembering the victory spirit Coach Bryant had helped instill in me.

As great a leader as Coach Bryant was, he also had a wonderful sense of humor. While he certainly had to know that he was one of the most successful football coaches in history and revered around (most of) Alabama, he was genuinely humble and even self-effacing. There was something about his folksy nature that humanized him and drew people in to him—a special kind of magnetism that is rare and that can't be manufactured.

In this book, I believe Richard Sikes has done a terrific job of pulling together dozens of short stories that paint a complete picture of this great man affectionately known as "the Bear." Some of these stories I have heard before, and some not, but all have succeeded in giving me another cherished ride down memory lane.

—*Jeff Rutledge*
Crimson Tide quarterback, 1975-78

Acknowledgments

Humorous columns by John Pruett of the *Huntsville Times* inspired me to first start thinking about doing this book, and Mr. Pruett provided a great deal of valuable advice about potential sources of "tales of the 'Bear'." Kirk McNair of *'Bama* magazine gave me a wealth of great information.

This book could not have been done without the support of the staff at the Paul W. Bryant Museum. A large debt of gratitude is owed to Clem Gryska, who coached for Coach Bryant for sixteen years and was full of "tales," as were former players Dennis Goehring and Baxter Booth.

My wife, Nell, was a patient and supportive advisor throughout the process, as was my son

Laughing with the Bear

Matthew (a fellow Tidesman), who was born twenty years too late to enjoy "Bear watching" firsthand.

Introduction:
The Bear Essentials

PAUL WILLIAM BRYANT was born September 11, 1913, in Moro Bottom, Arkansas. He was the eleventh of twelve children and was raised on an impoverished farm. To raise money, young Paul accompanied his mother into nearby Fordyce to sell milk, eggs, and vegetables from a mule-drawn wagon. The city slickers of Fordyce made fun of the young Bryant with his dusty overalls, bare feet, tired mules, and raggedy old wagon. Bryant attributed much of his later success in life to the fact that he was determined to work hard to ensure he would never again have to endure the taunts of the residents of his hometown.

When Paul was fourteen years old, a carnival that featured a wrestling bear came through Fordyce. The owner of the show promised to pay a dollar a minute to anyone who would wrestle the bear. A dollar a minute was a tremendous amount of money for a young boy accustomed to chopping cotton for fifty cents a day. So the strapping young Bryant quickly accepted the bear-wrestling challenge.

As the wrestling match began, Bryant's plan was to quickly charge the bear, take him down, and lay on top of the massive animal while the clock ticked on. However, the bear worked free of the teenager's grasp, and his muzzle came off. The unmuzzled animal bit Paul on the ear and blood gushed all over the stage of the theatre where the match was being staged. The sight of the blood frightened Bryant. He jumped from the stage and landed in the front row of seats. He quickly exited the building, and when he came back to collect his dollar, he discovered that the carnival operator was gone. He had left town. Although young Bryant never collected his money for wrestling the bear, he had earned a nickname that would stay with him for the rest of his life.

WHEN PAUL WAS in the eighth grade, the school football coach invited Bryant to try out for the local team. He quickly impressed the coach with his strength and aggressiveness. After the local cobbler nailed cleats onto his only pair of shoes, Bryant wound up playing in the first football game he ever saw. By the time he graduated from Fordyce High School, he had earned all-state honors as an end and was invited to play for the University of Alabama, recognized as the pre-eminent football power in the South after its Rose Bowl triumphs in the 1920s.

Although Bryant was a good football player at Alabama, he was destined to be known as "the other end" because he played at the same time as Don Hutson, one of football's all-time great pass catchers. After graduating from Alabama, Bryant landed an assistant-coaching job with the Crimson Tide. After a four-year stint as an assistant at his alma mater, he was offered a position on Red Sanders's staff at Vanderbilt and served in that role for two years. After the Japanese bombed Pearl Harbor, Bryant joined the navy and spent most of his military time coaching service football teams.

AFTER WORLD WAR II, Bryant got his first head-coaching position at the University of Maryland. Many of his former navy players followed him to College Park, and Bryant's 1945 Terrapins compiled a record of 6-2-1. Curly Byrd, University of Maryland president at the time and a former football coach, took it upon himself to offer coaching "suggestions" that were not enthusiastically received by the strong-willed Bear.

Byrd's hands-on tactics proved intolerable. While Bryant was out of town for the Christmas holidays after his first and only season with the Terps, Byrd fired one of Bear's assistant coaches and reinstated a player that Bryant had kicked off the team for drinking. When Bryant learned of Byrd's actions, he immediately resigned from Maryland even though he had no Plan B on which to fall back.

Within a few days of his resignation at Maryland, however, Coach Bryant was offered the head-coaching job at the University of Kentucky. When he accepted the Wildcats' job in January 1946, he took the helm of a program that had won a grand total of five Southeastern Conference games over the previous ten years. The eight years that Bryant coached the Wildcats were the school's most productive ever for a program that nonetheless continued to play second fiddle to the UK basketball program. Bryant's first team compiled a 7-3 record, and his 1950 squad won the only SEC football title in the school's history.

Although he compiled a record of 60-23-5 during his eight-year tenure in Lexington, Bryant eventually grew frustrated of running a football program in the shadow of Coach Adolph Rupp's ultra-successful hoops program. He left Kentucky when he thought that his football program would be hampered by NCAA restrictions imposed on the basketball program. Herman Edwards, University of Kentucky president at the time, promised Bryant that he would fire Coach Rupp because of the NCAA infractions. However, when the Bear saw a newspaper headline stating that Rupp had just signed a contract extension, the football coach resigned in a huff in February 1954.

The spur-of-the-moment resignation put Coach Bryant in the job market at an inopportune time. He had already turned down offers from football powers Southern Cal and Alabama following the 1953 season. The only vacant major-college job in February was with Texas A&M, an all-male military school.

A&M had suffered through mediocrity in the decade prior to Bryant's arrival. When the Bear got to College Station, he could not believe the low level of talent that he had inherited with the Aggies. Besides the lack of talent, the new coach soon realized that the team suffered from poor motivation and excessive meddling by A&M alumni ("the Aggie Exes"). To address these concerns, he arranged for an off-campus training camp in the drought-stricken, flyspeck town of Junction, Texas. What transpired next would become legend and the gist of a best-selling book, Jim Dent's *The Junction Boys*.

Bryant used Junction to identify a hard-nosed corps of players that he could count on to play hard to compensate for what they might be lacking in talent. He loaded two buses to transport 115 members of the football squad to Junction, and then a war of roster attrition started. After a hellish ten-day practice session, the thirty-five Junction "survivors" returned to the A&M campus in College Station on one bus.

Those surviving "Junction Boys" would win only one game against nine losses in 1954 to become what would be the only team with a losing record in Bryant's thirty-eight-year career as a head coach. It was a well-spent sacrifice, though. The sophomores who survived the hardnosed preseason camp would become the nucleus of A&M's 1957 Southwest Conference champions. Despite the 1954 Aggies' poor won-lost record, Bryant later said that the group was his all-time favorite team; and the majority of the Junction survivors attended an emotional twenty-fifth reunion in 1979. At the time of Coach Bryant's death in 1983, the only jewelry that he was wearing was the ring that he had been given by the Junction Boys at the reunion.

After struggling through that first year at Texas A&M, Coach Bryant's next three Aggie teams (1955–1957) compiled a 24-5-2 record. While he built the Aggies into a national power, his alma mater was experiencing some of the worst years in the history of their proud football program. Alabama coach J. B. "Ears" Whitworth won only four games from 1955 to 1957, and Tide supporters were calling for a return of the ex-Tidesman who was by now considered to be one of the nation's premier coaches. At the end of the 1957 season, Bryant heeded his "mama's call" and returned to Tuscaloosa to rebuild the Crimson Tide to the national prominence that they had enjoyed when he played for them in the early 1930s.

ALTHOUGH HE FACED a major rebuilding job at Alabama, as he had at his three previous schools, Coach Bryant quickly rebuilt the Crimson Tide program to a position of national prominence. His first recruiting class of 1958 won the national championship when they were seniors in 1961. His teams won six national championships and thirteen SEC championships during his twenty-five years at the Capstone. At the time of his retirement in 1982, Coach Bryant had won 323 games, more than any other coach in the history of college football at that time.

Since Bryant's death in January 1983 (one month after he coached his final game), his record for career victories has been surpassed by several others, but no other coach has risen to Bear's status as an authentic American legend. Bryant's legacy was as much the result of his outsized personality as it was of his remarkable won-lost record. He was more than a football coach; he was a larger-than-life American folk hero. One of the enduring memories football fans have of the Bear is the one of the houndstooth-hat-clad coach propped up against the goal post confidently watching his Crimson Tide execute their pregame drills. Whenever he entered a room, his charisma allowed him to become the center of attention even without saying a word.

Former Alabama player and assistant coach Jack Rutledge explained to Bryant biographer Keith Dunnavant that "Coach Bryant had a kind of magic to him. It was something that you really couldn't put your finger on, but you could feel it whenever he walked into the room." Long-time Penn State coach Joe Paterno said that the Bear had "tons of charisma" and described him as "a giant figure." One of the Bear's favorite quotes about himself was former Michigan State coach Duffy Daugherty's observation that "I don't know if the Bear is the best coach among us, but he sure causes the most commotion."

LAUGHING WITH THE BEAR

I.
YOUNG
BEAR

1
The Young Cub

A S A YOUNG BOY Bryant was extremely fearful of ghosts and tombstones. There was a graveyard about a hundred yards from his boyhood home, and as a youngster he would always avoid going near the side of the family farm where the graveyard was located. When Paul was about six or seven years old, his teenage brother Jack told him that he would give him fifty cents if he would walk up to a grave and slap the tombstone. Fifty cents was a lot of money in those days, and young Bryant decided that it was well worth it and that he would give it a try.

Jack watched as his younger brother tentatively approached the feared gravesite. Just as Paul reached out to slap the tombstone, a white form

3

popped out from behind the marker, startling Bryant. The frightened youngster forgot about the potential fifty cents and made a beeline for his house. When he slipped and fell as he was running home, he never even took time to get back up, and he crawled the rest of the way.

Paul later found out that the ghost had actually been a farmhand enticed by Jack to wear a sheet to play the prank on his younger brother. However, Paul got the last laugh as their mother made Jack pay his little brother the fifty cents anyway after she found out about the prank.

DURING HIS TEENAGE years, Paul gave his school-teachers fits. When he gave a woman teacher too much grief, she quit her job and was replaced by a man. The new teacher, Mr. Wysinger, quickly surmised that he would have to get Bryant's attention if he was going to maintain discipline in his class. During the new teacher's second day on the job, he gave young Paul a hard paddling. Bryant remarked to his schoolmates that when he grew up, he would whip Mr. Wysinger's butt. Word eventually got back to the teacher about the threats of his young student, but the teacher never said anything to the youngster.

Several years later, after he had graduated from high school, Bryant was hitchhiking back home from Tuscaloosa during college break. While walking down a dusty road near Fordyce, Bryant noticed an approaching Model-T Ford. He started to put his thumb out, but pulled it back when he realized it was his former teacher, Mr. Wysinger, pulling over to give him a ride. As he got into the car, Bryant remembered back to his school days and hoped that the teacher had forgotten that long-ago threat of retribution. After a few minutes of small talk, the teacher suddenly asked his former pupil if he remembered the threat he had made years before. Bryant sheepishly said that he did but that he still wasn't big enough to carry it out.

As he got into the car, Bryant remembered back to his school days and hoped that the teacher had forgotten that long-ago threat of retribution.

YOUNG BRYANT WAS not the most sophisticated collegian ever to arrive upon campus in Tuscaloosa. He was very self-conscious of his lack of polish, and his fellow students constantly made fun of their classmate. To help make sure that the poor native Arkansan had enough money to survive life away from home, the athletic department gave him a job cutting grass on the football field. Fellow football player Frank Howard, who was himself a resident of the metropolis of Barlow Bend, Alabama, once joked that it took the farm boy from Fordyce a month before he broke the habit of saying "gee, haw, and whoa" to the lawn mower.

2

The Bear in Love

A S YOUNG BRYANT developed an interest in the opposite sex, he reasoned that being a success in high school sports would make him more attractive to the female segment of the school's population. Both the Bear and Ike Murry, a teammate of his on the Fordyce High School Redbugs football team, were interested in impressing the same high school beauty. Murry, who would later serve as Arkansas attorney general, played center for the football team at the time that Paul was the star end.

One Friday night Fordyce was humiliating the high school team from Warren, Arkansas, leading, 58-0, with just a few minutes to play. The Redbugs had the ball on the Warren two-yard line and were poised to score yet another touchdown. It dawned on Bryant that the object of his affections would certainly be impressed if he could score a touchdown.

He talked his friend, quarterback Click Jordan, into trading places with him so that he would be in position to score the last touchdown. When Jordan announced his intentions in the huddle to trade places with Bryant, Murry knew what had instigated the change, and he was not about to assist his competitor in love. Murry said, "Like hell, that son-of-a-gun is not scoring any touchdowns while I'm centering." Jordan quelled the insurrection in the huddle, but as the team approached the line of scrimmage Murry mumbled to Bryant that "If you score, you'll be the first man to score a touchdown without having the ball."

As the team came up to the line of scrimmage, Bryant lined up in the quarterback position with his arms outstretched to receive the snap and score the much-anticipated touchdown. However, Murry's snap from center went over the new quarterback's head. By the time Bryant retrieved the ball, it had bounced and rolled all the way back to the forty-yard line, and his dreams of scoring one for his sweetheart were shattered.

3

So You Want to Quit?

W HILE FEELING UNAPPRECIATED as a player at Alabama, young Paul Bryant told several teammates that he was going to quit the team and probably transfer to LSU. This was not the first time that young Bryant had threatened to quit, and long-time Tide assistant coach Hank Crisp was determined to nip it in the bud.

The coach immediately sent for the disgruntled player and met with him in the equipment room. When Bryant arrived he found Coach Crisp holding a plow line that he was going to use to tie up the trunk in which the player kept his possessions. As Bryant approached him, Coach Crisp said, "I hear you want to leave. Well, damnit, I want you to leave, and I'm here to help you and make sure that you do. Come on, let's get that plow line out and tie this trunk up and get your butt out of here."

The reverse psychology worked, and the young Tidesman had to beg the coach to let him stay at Alabama.

4

The One-Legged Terror in Knoxville

WHILE PLAYING AGAINST Mississippi State the week before the Tide was to play Tennessee in 1935, Bryant broke the fibula in his right leg. On the night before the game against the Volunteers, the team physician came by the hotel where the Crimson Tide was staying in Knoxville and removed the cast from Bryant's leg.

Although he was obviously not expected to play against the Vols, young Bryant did dress for the game. Coach Frank Thomas made his pre-game pep talk, and then asked assistant coach Hank Crisp if he had anything to say. The assistant stood to address the team with a cigarette dangling from his mouth and said, "I don't know about the rest of you," as he pointed toward the team, "but I know one damn thing, old thirty-four will be after 'em, he'll be after their butts."

At that time the players generally changed numbers every week (to encourage fans to buy programs) and Bryant did not know who thirty-four was. When he looked down at his jersey, he was shocked to see that *he* was thirty-four. After that buildup it would have been impossible to have kept old number thirty-four out of the lineup, and the Bear had one of his best games ever as he led the Crimson Tide to a 25-0 victory over the Big Orange.

II.
OLD
KENTUCKY
HOME

5

Give the Boy
Some Coffee

DURING COACH BRYANT'S early years at Kentucky, many college students (including some of his football players) were returning war veterans who were older than their coach—who was then in his early thirties. When the 1946 Kentucky team was having its pregame dinner before the Tennessee game in Knoxville, the Bear asked the waiter for some coffee. The waiter told Bryant that he had been given instructions that the players could drink only tea or milk.

Bryant then told the waiter to never mind that, he wanted some coffee. At that point the waiter said he would have to check with the coach to see if it would be okay to serve him coffee. A grizzled war veteran named Bill Portwood, who was sitting next to the coach, then told the waiter, "It's all right, bring the boy some coffee."

6

Heavenly Recruiting

RECRUITING HAS ALWAYS been highly competitive, and Coach Bryant obviously had to be good at it in order to maintain the talent level necessary to have a topnotch football program. He frequently said that you could not make chicken salad if you did not have any chicken.

While Coach Bryant was coaching at Kentucky, there was a major recruiting battle for a high school hotshot named Gene Donaldson. Donaldson, a Catholic, was leaning to Notre Dame. However, Notre Dame coach Frank Leahy claimed that Bryant had arranged for Kentucky student manager Jim Murphy to pose as a priest to entice Donaldson to commit to the Wildcats. Bryant conceded that

"Maybe Jim Murphy did tell Donaldson he was a priest. Shucks, I'd have told him Murphy was Pope Pius if I'd thought we would get Donaldson that way."

WHEN HOWARD SCHNELLENBERGER was considered Kentucky's top high school lineman, the Louisville native verbally committed to Indiana University at the end of his senior year of high school. However, Coach Bryant recognized Schnellenberger's great potential and was not about to let him play outside the bluegrass state without a fight.

However, Coach Bryant recognized Schnellenberger's great potential and was not about to let him play outside the bluegrass state without a fight.

When the Bear first visited the Schnellenbergers' Louisville home, he had arranged for Kentucky governor Lawrence Wetherby to accompany him so as to impress the recruit and his parents. After a long sales pitch from Bryant and a sermon from the governor on Howard's duty to stay home and play for the state university, the young recruit was ready to rescind his verbal commitment to the Hoosiers and sign with the home-state Wildcats.

However, Mrs. Schnellenberger told her son that he had given his word to Indiana, and that he should honor his previous commitment. At that point Bryant realized that he had to change the mind of the mother. Several days after his first trip, Bryant showed up at the Schnellenberger house with the archbishop of the Louisville diocese of the Catholic Church. The archbishop then took the mother for a walk in the backyard. Mrs. Schnellenberger, a devout Catholic, was much more impressed by the cleric than she had been by the coach and the governor. When the mother and the priest came back into the living room, she told her son that the archbishop had convinced her that God would understand if he changed his mind.

Schnellenberger signed with Kentucky and was an outstanding lineman for the Wildcats. He was later a head coach at the University of Louisville, the University of Miami, and the University of Oklahoma.

7

The Bear
and the Baron

COACH BRYANT AND Kentucky basketball coach Adolph Rupp (the Baron of the Bluegrass) were both very successful, strong-willed individuals. Bryant found it hard to accept the fact that, in bluegrass country, his highly successful football program would always play second fiddle to the Baron's basketball program.

Throughout Bryant's stay at Kentucky, there were numerous reminders of the supremacy of the hoops program. In one of his first recruiting trips in the commonwealth, he went to Harrisburg to recruit a highly regarded football prospect. To get to Harrisburg, the coach had to drive all the way from East Chicago, Indiana, where he had had a speaking engagement the night before. He made the trip only because he had been assured that there would be a big crowd, and the local publicity in Harrisburg would be a boon to the football program.

Upon his arrival he realized that the promised "big crowd" consisted all of about twenty people. When the small-town mayor introduced Coach Bryant, he said, "I'm sorry we couldn't give Coach Bryant a key to the city, but we have given one to Coach Rupp for all the championships that he has won. We'll save one for when Coach Bryant wins as many games as Coach Rupp has won."

By the time the introduction was completed, the Bear was steaming. He stood up and said, "I don't want a key to the city. When I win as many games as Coach Rupp, I'll be able to buy the damn city and never even miss the money."

When the Kentucky football team won its first-ever Southeastern Conference title in 1950, the basketball team also won the conference title for the umpteenth time. After the season for both sports had ended, UK boosters had a triumphant banquet where they presented Rupp with a brand new blue Cadillac and gave Bryant a brand new Zippo cigarette lighter.

Years later, after Bryant had departed the bluegrass for Texas A&M and suffered through a one-victory season with the Aggies, he and Rupp both attended a coaching clinic in Utah. While addressing a group of sportswriters at the clinic, Rupp heaped praise on his former colleague. He said, "I want to tell you gentlemen something. Paul Bryant over there was at Kentucky, and he left us for a lot of money. You think he's down now, but I'll tell you, he will win. *He will win.* And you gentlemen in Texas who are playing him, he will run you right out of business. Five, ten years from now he *will* be the top man, make no mistake about it, and don't forget Uncle Adolph told you."

8

The Professors "Investigate" the Baron

THERE WAS SOME friction at the University of Kentucky between the academic side of the university and the highly successful football and basketball coaches. Coach Bryant was amused and impressed by the manner in which basketball coach Adolph Rupp handled a faculty group that was sent to investigate the athletic department.

The faculty group began their investigation by discussing finances and budgets with Coach Bryant. Then the academics proceeded next door to Uncle Adolph's office, where Coach Bryant said he could hear everything that was said as the professors conferred with the crusty old hoops coach. As the faculty representatives entered his office, Uncle Adolph greeted them with "By gad, come on in here! I've been waiting for you SOBs."

He called the name of one of his basketball players and asked one of the professors, "What the hell happened to my basketball player over there in your English class? By gad, you expect me to take these pine knots and make All Americans out of them, and I send you a B student and he's making a damned D." The poor professors were overwhelmed with Uncle Adolph's counteroffensive, and beat a hasty retreat out of his office before they even got around to *their* interrogation of the basketball coach.

9
Home for the Holidays

COACH BRYANT, WHO was in his thirties, was still in excellent physical condition while at Kentucky. He loved to give "hands-on" instruction to his players and could wreak major havoc on them with his forearms and elbows. One of his favorite live blocking dummies was All-American lineman Bob Gain. Although Gain was six-foot-four and weighed 235 pounds, he frequently came out second-best in head-to-head match-ups with his coach.

Bryant was known to be especially hard on his more talented players in order to motivate them to get the most out of their ability, and Gain was one of the most talented linemen that he ever coached. The massive lineman was not aware of Bryant's

After being humiliated one day on the practice field by his coach, a frustrated Gain, fed up with his treatment, decided that he was going over to Bryant's house to kick the coach's butt.

motivational approach and thought the coach just enjoyed banging him around. Gain prided himself on being one of the strongest and most physical players among the Wildcats, and he had a hard time accepting the fact that the coach could manhandle him physically.

After being humiliated one day on the practice field by his coach, a frustrated Gain, fed up with his treatment, decided that he was going over to Bryant's house to kick the coach's butt. As soon as Gain told his teammates what he was going to do, they started talking about wagering on the outcome of the teacher-pupil showdown. However, none of the players wanted to bet on Gain in the impending battle. Wildcat player Dude Hennessey said, "Everybody thought as I did that if they fought three times a day for a year, Bob would never whip Coach Bryant."

On the night of the confrontation, a contingent of curious players went over to the Bryant house and peered out from the shrubbery to watch the much-anticipated showdown. They saw Gain finally work up enough courage to approach the front door.

After the player knocked on the door, the coach answered and asked, "What the hell do you want, Gain?" After hesitating for a few seconds, the massive lineman stammered: "Coach, some of the guys were wondering if you were going to let us go home for Christmas break."

10
Good for the Goose and the Gander

C OACH BRYANT WAS a stickler for being on time for team meetings and practice sessions. During preseason practice at Kentucky, a player (and later a Bryant assistant coach) named Pat James showed up thirty minutes late for practice one day because he had spent too much time at the local fishing hole between the morning and afternoon sessions.

When James finally arrived at practice, he took his spot on the squad just as if nothing had happened. Nobody said anything. When practice was over, Coach Bryant told James that before he arrived for practice a kangaroo court had decided that, as punishment for being late, he would have to clean up all the piles of manure from a cow pasture adjoining the football field. James then dutifully covered up all the manure piles with sand.

The next day the trainer failed to awaken Coach Bryant in time for the morning practice, and he arrived thirty minutes late. After practice ended, James went over to the coach, and said that the kangaroo court had met again and had decided that since *he* was late for practice he should go over and clean the manure out of the field. The Bear spent the next two hours cleaning the field out.

III.
AGGIE TIME

11

Sleeping in Church

A FTER A WEEK of brutal workouts in intolerably hot and dry weather at Junction, Texas, the 1954 edition of the Texas A&M Aggies were relieved when Coach Bryant called them together on a Saturday afternoon and asked how many of the players wanted to go to church in Junction on Sunday. Whether they were religious or not, all forty of the remaining players raised their hands because they saw this as a chance to get a short respite from the grueling practice schedule they had endured since their arrival at the off-campus hellhole.

However, the expectations of a Sunday break were quickly dispelled at 5:30 on Sunday morning. Players were awakened by the sounds of the whistles of the student managers sent by Bryant to get them ready for a pre-church workout. It was only after the completion of an intense three-hour practice session that the players were able to get ready for church.

When the exhausted players finally arrived at the First Baptist Church of Junction, the entire group sat in the last three pews. As the singing began, Bryant sang along without ever opening a hymn book as he was thoroughly familiar with the old hymns of the church.

After the first song ended, the coach turned around to check on the condition of his players. When he looked, he saw that all forty of his players were sound asleep. Each player had his head propped up on the shoulder of the teammate to his right. The combination of the cool air and soothing music had caused the exhausted players to fall fast asleep.

12
You Can't Run Me Off

A FTER ARRIVING AT Texas A&M, Coach Bryant soon realized that his first Aggie team would be woefully short of talent. His famous off-campus, pre-season training camp at the remote Texas town of Junction was an attempt to mold the talent that he did have available into the very best possible team. It was critical that the members of the coaching staff focus their attention on the best prospects and not waste time on players who had little chance of helping the team.

One of the Aggies that the coaching staff concluded was unlikely to be a contributor to the team was a small, slow, and seemingly untalented guard named Dennis Goehring. Since Goehring had been classified as a probable noncontributor, the coaching staff did everything possible to encourage him to quit so they would have more time to develop players who had more potential. It quickly became evident to Goehring what the coaches were trying to do, and he had no intention of quitting because his football scholarship was his only hope of getting a college education.

Goehring, only five-foot-ten and 180 pounds, started practice as the seventh team right guard. During the rugged practices, he was regularly pounded by his bigger and more talented teammates. However, the scrappy little lineman had nothing else to fall back on, and he was determined that they were not going to make him quit.

After one particularly rugged Junction practice session, Smokey Harper, the crusty old A&M trainer who had previously been with Bryant at Kentucky, approached Goehring. Harper asked the lineman, "Why don't you just give it up? You're never gonna make it." The reply from the exhausted Goehring was a classic. He looked the old trainer squarely in the eye and said, "I'll be here long after you and Bryant are both gone."

When Harper related that conversation to Bryant, the demanding coach could not suppress a grin. He knew he had identified a player who at least had the spirit of a champion. In his senior season in 1956, Goehring became an All American. And true to his word, he did outlast both his coach and trainer in College Station. He eventually became president of a bank in the college town.

At the twenty-fifth reunion of the Junction Boys in 1979, the banker, by now a millionaire, told his cohorts of a recent show of support from his old coach. In the early 1970s Goehring had decided to increase his bank's capitalization by selling stock in the institution. He immediately thought of his old, wealthy mentor as a potential investor but was apprehensive about approaching him. Finally, the banker summoned the courage to call Bryant.

After opening the conversation with small talk, Goehring worked up enough courage to ask his old coach to buy two hundred shares of stock. After the request was made, the banker heard nothing but silence on the other end of the phone line. As the silence seemed to last

After opening the conversation with small talk, Goehring worked up enough courage to ask his old coach to buy two hundred shares of stock. After the request was made, the banker heard nothing but silence on the other end of the phone line.

an eternity, the banker thought that maybe he should have asked Bryant to sign up for only a hundred shares. Finally, the gruff voice on the other end responded: "Hell, Dennis, I don't want two hundred shares. I've got more confidence in you than that. Give me a thousand shares."

13
Recruiting Aggies

T O SAY THAT Coach Bryant's predecessor at Texas A&M, Ray George, had left the talent cupboard bare is an understatement. The new Aggie mentor was stunned by the dearth of talent when he studied the films of the 1953 Aggie season. The A&M players that he had inherited had nowhere near the talent level that he had left behind at Kentucky. After guiding the Aggies through their spring drills in 1954, he was even more discouraged about the upcoming season.

During the summer, the Bear dispatched assistant coach Elmer Smith to Alabama to try to find some players. After watching an all-star game featuring recently graduated high school seniors in

Birmingham, Coach Smith was pessimistic when he called his boss back at College Station. When Coach Bryant inquired if there were *any* unsigned players who could help the Aggies, Smith replied that there was one. When Bryant then told Smith to go ahead and sign the lone prospect to a scholarship, the assistant coach replied, "Well, there is one thing about him—he only has one arm."

That player was Murry Trimble, who would go on to become an all-conference guard at A&M, and whose brother Wayne played for Bryant at Alabama in the 1960s.

Bryant was constantly hounded by A&M alumni (referred to as Aggie exes) who considered themselves key elements in A&M's imminent return to pigskin glory. His decision to hold his preseason 1954 training camp off campus in remote Junction was partially the result of his desire to escape the "assistance" of the exes.

In his first meeting with the alumni after taking the A&M job, Bryant minced no words in explaining how he interpreted the relationship between the head coach and the boosters. To make sure there were no misunderstandings he said, "Up to now there have been too many chiefs and not enough Indians around here. From now on I'm the chief and you're the Indians. I know how to coach football. You may *think* you know how, but I *know* I do, so I don't need your advice."

Within the first couple of weeks after his arrival at College Station, Bryant saw an Aggie booster from Palestine, Texas, drive up in a big black Cadillac. The Aggie exe swaggered into the coach's office with five "prospects" trailing along behind. The Bear had already dispatched Coach Smith to east Texas where Palestine was located, and Smith had informed Bryant that there were no potential recruits in the area. Bryant quickly assessed the potential talent of the "prospects" and informed the booster, "If thin shoulders and a skinny tail will get the job done, you've got five All Americans."

After delivering that assessment to the free-lance recruiter, Bryant turned and walked away. He never saw the man again.

14
The Mustard Seed

C OACH BRYANT'S FIRST Texas A&M team opened
the 1954 season with a blowout 41-9 loss to
Texas Tech. Even though A&M won only one of its
next six games, they did show vast improvement from
their opening-game performance as the average margin of defeat in those five losses was only six points.
However, the eighth game of the season was against
a strong Southern Methodist University team, and
Bryant feared that he would suffer another embar-
rassing blowout loss if he could not find a way to
motivate his underdog Aggies.

When the coach discussed his dilemma with his
assistant coaches, long-time assistant Elmer Smith
recounted an experience where his college coach had

motivated his team by using the saying in the Bible that you could move a mountain if you had faith as big as a grain of mustard seed.

Coach Bryant listened to Smith's suggestion but did not tell a soul about his intentions. At midnight on Thursday before the SMU game, he called all of the assistant coaches and told them to meet him at the team dormitory at 1:00 A.M. When the assistants arrived, he told them to go get the players for a "prayer session." The coaches went from room to room rousing the sleeping players for the surprise team meeting.

When the assistants arrived, he told them to go get the players for a "prayer session." The coaches went from room to room rousing the sleeping players for the surprise team meeting.

Dennis Goehring recounted that when assistant coach Willie Zapalac awoke him in the wee hours of the morning he initially thought Zapalac was a teammate who was playing a prank, and the coach narrowly averted being hit over the head with a pillow. The sleepy players thought that a prayer meeting with Bryant would be somewhat out of character for their hard-nosed mentor. They were further amused when they saw the coach fumble through the Bible trying to find the mustard seed verse. He was unable to find the verse in the Bible and instead paraphrased it as he gave each one a mustard seed encapsulated in plastic. The coach then said, "Gentlemen, life's battles don't always go to the stronger or faster man. Sooner or later the man who wins is the man who thinks he can." Then the coach turned around and walked out of the room.

At that point, the Bear had no idea whether his gimmick would work or backfire. However, that Saturday's performance against a talented SMU team was A&M's best of the season, and the Aggies lost by the narrow margin of 6-3.

Years later long-time friend and Texas coach Darrell Royal called and told Coach Bryant he was looking for a way to motivate his undefeated Longhorns before an important game against persistent nemesis Rice University. Coach Bryant said there were no surefire ways to motivate a team but told him about his experiences with the mustard seed. After hearing the results that Bryant had gotten from the mustard seed story, Royal said he would try it, too.

When Coach Bryant opened his Sunday paper that week he was anxious to see if the mustard seed gimmick had worked for his pal. When he found the score in the paper it was Rice 34, Texas 7.

15
Poor Henry

I N 1955 COACH BRYANT coached a game for the first time in his home state of Arkansas since he had left for Tuscaloosa as a seventeen-year-old in 1930. His Texas A&M team of that year was dramatically improved over his 1954 "Junction Boys," and he was determined to make a triumphant return to his home state. The Aggies entered the game undefeated in Southwest Conference play, and although Arkansas had only a 3-3 record they were the defending SWC champions. An Aggie win in Fayetteville would send a signal that the Texas A&M program had turned the corner under its second-year coach.

The first half of the game ended in a scoreless tie as a hardnosed Razorback defense shut down John

David Crow, the star Aggie running back, and completely thwarted the three different quarterbacks that Bryant used to try to generate some offense.

At halftime Bryant was determined to get the team fired up to play a better second half. He went from locker to locker scolding the players. As he approached guard Dennis Goehring he implored him, "Goehring, you SOB, you block somebody."

Bryant favorite Gene Stallings was greeted with "Stallings, some days I like you. Some days I don't. Get your head out of your butt."

Crow was told, "Damnit, you're spending too much time reading your own press clippings."

Massive sophomore lineman Charlie Krueger was challenged with, "Krueger, I can't believe a boy your size is getting pushed around by these little-bitty boys."

Then the coach went to tackle Henry Clark and picked him up by his shoulder pads and shook him like a sack of potatoes. As he shook the chunky Clark, Bryant told him, "Henry, you let that man shoot the gap on you one more time and you'll walk all the way back to Texas." The bewildered tackle looked at Bryant and said in a high-pitched voice, "Coach, I ain't even been in the game yet."

16
Running for His Life

T HE TEXAS A&M AGGIES played their Southwest Conference rival the Arkansas Razorbacks every year, and this was always a big game for Coach Bryant, a native Arkansan. He was always anxious for his team to look good before the home folks. When they played in Fayetteville in 1957, the Aggies had the added incentive of needing a victory to keep alive their aspirations of defending the conference championship that they had won the year before.

The 1957 encounter was a hard-fought defensive struggle, and the Aggies were desperately clinging to a 7-6 lead with only twenty-eight seconds left to play. A&M had the ball on the Arkansas thirty-five-yard line, and Bryant sent in a play in which

Suddenly, an Arkansas defensive back named Donny Horton, who was also a sprinter on the Razorbacks' track team, came out of nowhere and picked off Osborne's pass.

quarterback Roddy Osborne would roll out around end and eat up as much time as possible to insure the victory. Although it was an option pass play, where one receiver went out for a pass and everybody else blocked for the quarterback, it was understood that under no circumstances was Osborne going to risk a pass.

As the quarterback started to roll out, he cocked his arm and acted like he was going to pass to Heisman Trophy winner John David Crow, who appeared to be wide open. At that point Osborne tried to heave a little shot-put-type toss to the wide-open Crow. Suddenly, an Arkansas defensive back named Donny Horton, who was also a sprinter on the Razorbacks' track team, came out of nowhere and picked off Osborne's pass.

The only person between the speedy Horton and the game-winning touchdown was Osborne, one of the slowest runners on the entire A&M team. Miraculously, Osborne was able to overtake his much-faster rival, and he tackled him near the Aggie thirty-yard line. Three plays later Crow intercepted an Arkansas pass in the end zone to preserve the win.

Several days later Coach Bryant told Georgia Tech Bobby Dodd about the incident during a telephone call. Dodd said he could not understand how a player as slow as Osborne could have run down a speed demon like Horton. Bryant's explanation was simple: "The difference is that Horton was running for a touchdown. Osborne was running for his life."

17
The Chief
and the Indians

THROUGHOUT HIS COACHING career, Coach Bryant was known for having some of the best assistant coaches in all of college football. Assistant coaches were always eager to learn from "the master," and a large number of his assistants went on to become head coaches at other schools. Although he had a good working relationship with his assistants, the head coach with the oversized ego always maintained the proper distance from his subordinates.

One of Coach Bryant's most energetic assistant coaches was Pat James. James had played for the Bear at Kentucky and then served as an assistant coach for him at Kentucky, Texas A&M, and Alabama. While James was serving as an assistant at Texas A&M, the coaching staff discussed moving a player named Patterson from guard to center. After afternoon practice had ended, the coaches showered, dressed, and were preparing to go home.

As Coach Bryant was walking out of the door of the dressing room, he said that he had moved Patterson. Upon hearing this news, James said in a flip tone of voice, "I'll buy that." Bryant reopened the door to the dressing room and stuck his nose back in and said, "I don't give a damn if you buy it or not," and he then slammed the door again. Assistant coach Elmer Smith said that James then got up to make sure that Bryant had left and then got down in a lineman's stance and said, "One of these days I'm going home and lock myself in the closet and cuss the hell out of that SOB."

ONE OF COACH BRYANT'S favorite assistants was O. E. "Bum" Phillips who served on his staff at A&M and would later become head coach of the Houston Oilers and later the New Orleans Saints. During Bum's first practice with the Aggies, he was instructed to get to practice fifteen minutes early to work with the quarterbacks and the centers.

When Coach Bryant arrived at practice that day, Phillips was already there. When Bum realized that there were no footballs out on the practice field, he approached Bryant and asked him if the student managers would have the footballs out on the field on time. The Bear grinned as he told Phillips, "I don't know, Bum, but I'll tell you one damn thing. I ain't gonna go get them."

BILL OLIVER, A player and assistant football coach for Bryant at Alabama, and assistant Alabama basketball coach Wimp Sanderson were roommates at a two-day golf outing that Coach Bryant hosted in the early seventies. After showering following a round of golf on the first day of the outing, Sanderson discovered that their bathroom had no towels. He asked Oliver to "run next door and grab a couple of towels." Oliver then asked Sanderson if he knew who was staying next door. When Oliver then explained that Coach Bryant was their next-door neighbor, Sanderson said, "Forget it then. We've got plenty of toilet paper."

IV.
HOME AT THE CAPSTONE

18
Help from
the Domino Club

DURING THE EXTREMELY unsuccessful tenure of J. B. "Ears" Whitworth as Alabama's football coach, every Wednesday was designated as dominoes day. On that day several former Crimson Tide players would come by Whitworth's office to play a few games of dominoes, discuss the progress (or lack of progress) of the football team, and tell the coach what he was doing wrong.

Long-time 'Bama assistant coach Clem Gryska surmised that since Whitworth only won four games in three years, the discussions of what he was doing wrong could have been rather lengthy. Sometimes the discussions lasted past lunchtime, and they would send out for sandwiches.

Whitworth apparently enjoyed both the company and the assistance.

Shortly after Coach Bryant succeeded Whitworth as coach of the Tide in January 1958, the domino crowd stopped by to see him. They informed the Bear that they were willing to help him whip the team into shape, play a few games of dominoes, and discuss strategy with the coach. The domino clubbers apparently were not familiar with Bryant's reputation, or they would have known that he was not disposed to using "consultants" to help him run his football program.

Bryant told them that he did not have time to see them then, but he would be glad to set up an appointment to talk to them at 5:30 the next morning. This treatment thoroughly angered the would-be Bryant assistants, and they stomped off down the hall of the athletic department and never offered to "help" the ungrateful Bear again.

19
You Need a New Car

THE ONLY PERSON from "Ears" Whitworth's Alabama football staff retained by Coach Bryant was trainer Jim Gostree. Between the preseason morning and afternoon practice sessions, the coach and the trainer would frequently walk from the athletic department offices to Druid Drugstore in Tuscaloosa to get a cup of coffee. One afternoon it started raining just before the twosome began their trip to the drugstore, and Coach Bryant suggested that they ride there in Gostree's car.

Gostree's car was considerably less than a limousine. He drove an old 1950 Chevrolet (this was in 1958) that he had bought for seventy-five dollars the previous year. The car had been painted with a brush, and the left front door would not open. Therefore, the driver had to get into the vehicle on the passenger side, and close the right door with a wire before getting behind the steering wheel.

Gostree had planned to walk to the drugstore in the rain rather than give his boss a ride in his jalopy. But once the Bear suggested they ride, the trainer was not about to refuse his boss's request.

The Bear, all six feet four inches of him, had to scrunch up to ride in the old Chevy. The ride was uneventful if not exactly comfortable for the coach.

As they approached the car, Gostree explained to Coach Bryant that the driver would have to get in first and then the passenger. The Bear, all six feet four inches of him, had to scrunch up to ride in the old Chevy. The ride was uneventful if not exactly comfortable for the coach. However, when they arrived at the drugstore, Coach Bryant started to get out of the car, only to step down on Gostree's floorboard, which had rusted out and was covered with cardboard. At that point the coach's foot went all the way through the floorboard to the ground. When he raised his leg back through the collapsed floorboard, his shin was soaked in blood.

The two men then went into the drugstore and had their coffee. When they came out to begin the return trip to the athletic offices, the rain was still pouring down. Coach Bryant looked at the car and then at the sky. Then he told Gostree, "I believe I'll walk back to the office."

20
Who Hired that Idiot?

D URING THE LAST three years of Coach Bryant's tenure at Texas A&M, the Alabama Crimson Tide was putting together its worst record ever under the tutelage of J. B. Ears" Whitworth. Whitworth had played at the Capstone in the 1930s, and he had been the head coach at Oklahoma A&M before becoming head man at 'Bama in 1955. However, his record of four victories in three years indicated that he was not cut out to be a head coach. As it became clear that Whitworth was not going to lead the Crimson Tide to their accustomed success on the gridiron, a search committee was formed to find "the finest football coach in the country."

One of the most influential members of the search committee was Montgomery businessman Winton "Red" Blount, who would later become United States postmaster general. Blount, who had himself been a high school football star (and thus was very knowledgeable in all aspects of the game), took considerable pride in letting his friends know that he had been influential in luring the coaching genius from College Station to Tuscaloosa.

Blount invited a large entourage to Starkeville to watch Coach Bryant's first Alabama team play Mississippi State in the fifth game of the 1958 season. He planned to take his share of the credit for recruiting the genius who was coaching the Crimson Tide. However, in Bryant's first season at the Capstone, his team suffered from a lack of talent that was a leftover from Whitworth's poor recruiting. Therefore, the Bear was forced to play "gimmick football" to even stay on the field with a Mississippi State team that was picked by some experts to win the SEC championship.

Mississippi State took the opening kickoff and put a scare into Blount and his colleagues as the Bulldogs drove to the Alabama six-yard line. However, when the Tide stopped State and took possession of the ball, Red smiled knowingly at his compatriots. On first down Tide halfback Gary O'Steen unleashed a quick kick that traveled seventy yards to the Bulldogs' twenty-four-yard line. This confusing strategic move caused Blount to ask, "What's going on?"

State then took the ball and marched down to the 'Bama fifteen before the Tide dug in and stopped them again. The Tide then picked up nine rushing yards on first down which led to hearty cheers from the Blount portion of the 'Bama cheering section. On the next play Alabama launched another quick kick that rolled all the way to the State twenty-yard line. At that point Blount was starting to get frustrated and he griped, "How are you gonna win kicking all the time?"

State then took the ball and drove back to the Tide twelve-yard line before the 'Bama defense again stiffened and stopped the Bulldogs' advance. Alabama then made a first down on their first play and Blount told everybody he was starting to feel a lot better about how his team was being coached. On the very next play, though, O'Steen quick kicked again and Red jumped out of his seat and yelled "Hell's bells. We've done hired ourselves an idiot."

O'Steen's numerous quick kicks proved to be the difference in the game as Alabama defeated

Mississippi State, 9-7, despite being substantially out-gained by the Bulldogs. After the game Blount called Coach Bryant on the phone and said, "Bear, I just want you to know that I don't understand what you're doing, but whatever it is, I'm for it."

21
Hold that Line—Or Else

ALTHOUGH ALABAMA HAD won only four games in the three years before Coach Bryant returned to Tuscaloosa to revitalize the Tide football program in 1958, the Bryant-led Tide played *almost* as well as hard core 'Bama fans had hoped for early in the coach's inaugural season.

After the first six games of the year, the Crimson Tide had compiled a record of 3-2-1, and there was talk that a strong finish could earn a bowl trip. There was a feeling of optimism in the air as the Tide prepared for their seventh game of the year against Tulane in New Orleans. The Green Wave had won only two of their first seven games, and Alabama supporters were confident that their team would leave the Big Easy with their fourth victory of the year. However, the Crimson Tide, seemingly out of sync throughout the game, had two touchdowns called back against Tulane because of penalties and were defeated, 13-7. Before the game, Coach Bryant had promised the players that they would be allowed some time in the French Quarter after the Friday night game. However, after the disappointing loss, their "tour" of the French Quarter consisted of a short bus trip through it on the way back to their hotel.

Before the game, Coach Bryant had promised the players that they would be allowed some time in the French Quarter after the Friday night game.

Missing out on the New Orleans nightlife turned out to be a blessing because the players were awakened at 5:00 A.M. the next morning and told to pack for the flight back to Alabama. When they arrived in Tuscaloosa, buses were waiting to take them directly to the practice field. The Saturday practice was the first in a series of tough sessions leading up to the next game versus Georgia Tech in Atlanta. The players also endured a 9:00 A.M. practice on Sunday and extremely tough sessions throughout the week that emphasized a Bryant-style "return to fundamentals."

Georgia Tech, at 5-2-1, was an obvious favorite over the Crimson Tide. Tech was touted as being both bigger and faster than the Tide, and the Ramblin' Wreck was confident that a win over 'Bama would lock up their own invitation to the Gator Bowl. Bryant and Tech coach Bobby Dodd were long-time friends and the Bear wanted his team to play well against the Engineers. It quickly became obvious that Alabama had come to play as they broke out to a 17-0 lead by the end of the first half.

However, the Tide fumbled the ball away on the second play of the second half, and Tech recovered it on the 'Bama twenty-seven-yard line. The Engineers quickly moved the ball to the Tide two-yard line. At that point Bryant was concerned that a quick touchdown would put the talented Yellow Jackets right back into the game. He sent a message to his defense that if they did not stop Tech, there would be a repeat of the seven-day-a-week practice sessions that had followed the Tulane game. This motivation worked wonders as Alabama stuffed the Tech offense with a magnificent goal line stand, and after four Tech plays the Tide took possession of the ball on their own three-yard line and went on to win the game.

22

Firing the Quarterback

T HE 1960 GAME with Georgia Tech in Atlanta was one of the most memorable games in Alabama Crimson Tide history. It was played in the third year after Coach Bryant returned to Tuscaloosa to resurrect the football fortunes of his alma mater. The fact that it occurred against one of the Tide's traditional rivals and another long-time Southern football power made the victory even sweeter for Tide fans. Coach Bryant described it as one of the greatest comebacks with which he had ever been involved.

The Georgia Tech Yellow Jackets were coached by Bobby Dodd, widely respected as one of the best coaches in the South as well as the nation. At that time Dodd's teams were consistently in the national rankings and making numerous bowl appearances. Although 1960 was Coach Bryant's third year at Alabama, the Tide had not reached the status of consistent national power that they would achieve later in his tenure.

The Tide started the game slowly against the more talented Yellow Jackets and were behind, 15-0, at the half. They did not even make a first down until the last play before halftime. The Alabama players feared a strong tongue lashing from Bryant at halftime after this lackluster first-half performance. The coach was undecided how to handle the halftime discussion as he headed to the dressing room. Being a master psychologist, he feared that his usual ranting and raving would only dispirit the team and lead to a blowout loss in the second half.

As the apprehensive players and assistant coaches filed into the dressing room, Coach Bryant sat for a long time calmly smoking a cigarette. Finally, he said, "Where are the Cokes? Let's get some Cokes in here." Then the Coach started walking around the locker room patting the players on the back and saying, "Damn, this is great. Now they'll see what kind of mamas and papas we've got. They'll see what we've got in us."

The Alabama assistant coaches and players could not believe their ears. Assistant coach Clem Gryska said that everyone was shocked by the coach's friendly approach because they were expecting to be reamed out. Instead, Coach Bryant calmly went to the chalkboard and drew up a couple of plays and said that if he had done as good a job as the players had, they wouldn't be in the position they were in. He said he wasn't concerned because they were still going to win. He said that he had screwed up a couple of things in the first half, but if they would help him get things straightened out they would win the game in the fourth quarter. Coach Bryant said in his autobiography that *he* didn't believe that they would win, but the players sure did.

Sure enough, the Tide did start playing better in the second half, although they were still unable to score in the third quarter and began the final quarter still down, 15-0. As the fourth quarter began, they faced a fourth-and-twelve situation from their own six-yard line. At that point the Tide coach thought it was time to shake things up, so he surprised everyone when he decided to go for the first down rather than punt.

Bryant sent in a play that consisted of a fifteen-yard buttonhook pass pattern that would get the much-needed first down. Bobby Skelton, who was then playing quarterback, misunderstood the play call that had been sent in from the bench and mistakenly called a six-yard hook pass. Even if the pass had been successful, Alabama would have still been short of the first down. Skelton then proceeded to throw an interception right to a defensive lineman for the Yellow Jackets.

At that point Bryant yanked Skelton out of the lineup. The coach said he felt like he could have bitten Skelton's helmet when he came to the sideline.

At that point Bryant yanked Skelton out of the lineup. The coach said he felt like he could have bitten Skelton's helmet when he came to the sideline.

The irate Bryant greeted the quarterback with a few choice words as he approached the bench, and then told him that he would never play another minute for the Crimson Tide as long as he lived. Bryant prided himself on having resourceful quarterbacks, and he said he got so upset at Skelton because he called the wrong play—not because he threw the interception.

Miraculously, Alabama's defense kept Georgia Tech from scoring, and when the Tide regained possession, junior quarterback Pat Trammell replaced Skelton in the lineup. Trammell gave the Crimson Tide decent field position by completing a thirty-yard pass on the first play after he replaced Skelton. However, Trammell twisted his ankle on the next play and hobbled to the sideline. Now, the Bear was in a perilous situation since he had one quarterback who could barely walk and one whom he had just "fired."

At that point Coach Bryant became pragmatic. He approached Skelton on the sideline and told him that he was going to give him one more chance. With six minutes left to play, the comeback began. Skelton converted four times on fourth down on the first touchdown drive. After the touchdown, Alabama kicked the extra point to cut Tech's lead to 15-7.

Then the Tide successfully executed an onsides kick and promptly scored another touchdown. However, they failed to make the two-point conversion try and trailed, 15-13, with slightly more than two minutes to play. Now everybody expected 'Bama to try another onsides kick, but instead they kicked the ball out of the end zone and Tech took over on its own twenty-yard line. The Crimson Tide defense held, and by using all of their timeouts they were able to take possession of the ball on their own forty-five yard line after returning the Yellow Jacket punt. There was now less than a minute to play.

Skelton immediately hit Butch Wilson with a thirty-three yard pass that should have been ruled incomplete because Wilson had been bumped out of bounds as he ran his pattern. However, the officials didn't notice that Wilson had gone out of bounds, and 'Bama was now in field-goal range.

Unfortunately, the Tide's regular kicker, Tommy Brooker, was standing on the sideline on crutches. The second-string kicker, a seldom used end named Richard "Digger" O'Dell, had never even attempted a field goal in a game. Coach Bryant walked over and calmly told O'Dell, "Get on out there, Digger, and kick one." O'Dell responded with a knuckleball of a kick that seemed to graze the cross-bar as it went through the uprights. A stunned silence fell over the Grant Field crowd, as 'Bama had pulled off the incredible come-from-behind upset.

23

The Pygmy and the Giant

I N THE FIRST FEW years after Bryant returned to Alabama, his teams were known for being considerably smaller than their opponents. They typically weighed anywhere from ten to thirty pounds per man less than the opposition, but their quickness allowed them to compensate for their lack of size.

One Friday in the early sixties, long-time Southeastern Conference officials Butch Lambert and Harold Johnson got into a conversation about Bryant's uncanny ability to win games with such small players as they drove to that week's Crimson Tide game. Johnson told Lambert that he thought that Coach Bryant could teach a four-foot pygmy to guard Wilt Chamberlain (the giant seven-foot-two basketball star).

The next day, when Lambert saw Bryant in the Alabama dressing room before the game, the official approached the coach and told him that Johnson had given him a great compliment. When the coach inquired what the compliment was, Lambert told him about the Chamberlain comment. Bryant, preoccupied with getting ready for the upcoming game, simply told Lambert, "Hell, Butch, I don't know anything about coaching basketball."

Lambert then went over and began a conversation with Alabama assistant coach Dude Hennessey. The conversation abruptly ended as Lambert felt a tap on his shoulder. As the official turned around, he saw Coach Bryant grinning as he towered over him. Bear then remarked to Lambert, "That ain't to say that ole SOB can't be guarded."

24

No Springs—Honest Weight

COACH BRYANT'S EARLY Alabama teams were known for their small size, quickness, and ferocity on defense. He was proud of the way his "little bitty" boys could embarrass their much-larger opponents. Even though the Tidesmen were smaller than their opponents, the Bear also consciously understated his players' weights in an attempt to "poor mouth" his team's chances.

Clemson coach Frank Howard was as colorful a personality as Bryant was, and he could hold his own against the Bear when it came to "poor mouthing." Bryant and Howard were long-time friends and had been teammates in the 1930s at Alabama. As the 1966 Clemson-Alabama game in Tuscaloosa approached,

Howard decided to let the Bear know that he was not fooled by the understated weights for the Crimson Tide players. He said that he was not about to be misled "by old 'Beah' down there lying about those skinny little boys of his, all supposed to weigh 180."

Charley Thornton, the sports information director for the Tide at that time, related how Bryant tried to "prove" the accuracy of his scales to the suspicious Howard. Thornton, Clemson SID Bob Bradley, and the Bear set up an elaborate practical joke on Howard. First, they had the scales "fixed" so that their reading was thirty pounds less than the actual weight. Then Bryant had Thornton take a signed copy of the team roster to a notary who "certified" it as accurate. Of course, all that the notary certified was that the signature was of the person signing the document and not the accuracy of the players' weights.

On the Friday before the game, Bryant asked Howard to come by his office before the Tigers conducted their daily workout. Frank suspected that he was being set up but did not know how. The Bear first presented Howard with the "certified" roster weights. Then Bryant took him to the rigged scales and told him, "This is where we weigh our players, and I want you to be satisfied that our figures are right." Then

Bear asked Bradley how much he weighed and Bradley subtracted thirty pounds from his weight and said about 137. Bradley got on the scales, and sure enough they registered 137. Next, Thornton was asked how much he weighed and he also subtracted thirty pounds from his weight and said about 132. Sure enough, the scales showed that Thornton weighed in the low 130s.

When Bear told Howard to get on the scales, the needle settled at about 225. Frank had not weighed 225 since his teenage days but he told Bryant, "Beah, I owe you an apology. Them scales are right on the money."

25
Helping the Hoopsters

A FTER HE HAD BUILT a solid foundation for the Alabama football program, Athletic Director Bryant decided to upgrade the basketball program after Coach Hayden Riley retired in 1967. Former Kentucky player C. M. Newton was highly recommended as an up-and-coming young coach, and he was hired to lift the 'Bama hoops program to a position of national prominence. Coach Newton's program had reached the point where the Tide was invited to the National Invitation Tournament in New York in 1973 (the NIT was a considerably more prestigious tournament in 1973 than it is today).

When the team journeyed to the Big Apple to participate in the NIT, Coach Newton invited his football coach to make the trip with them. Although NCAA rules strictly limit who can sit on a college team's bench during a game, the basketball coach did not have the heart to refuse Coach Bryant's request to sit with the Crimson Tide. After telling Coach Newton of his plans to join the team on the bench, Bryant also informed the basketball coach that he had invited long-time friend Sonny Werblin (who ran Madison Square Garden) to also sit on the bench.

Coach Bryant was an enthusiastic though not an especially knowledgeable roundball fan. He constantly complained to the referees about the fouls (which he called "penalties") that were called on the Tide. When a ball headed toward the Bear on the 'Bama bench, he instinctively caught the ball even though it was still in play. Normally, that would have resulted in a technical foul being called on the bench, but the referee merely explained to Coach Bryant that he should not touch a ball that was still in play.

When Alabama finished the game with a one-point victory over Manhattan, the local team was dismayed as they saw the referees go over to the Tide bench for an autograph from the legendary football coach.

26
Welcome to Knoxville

ALABAMA-TENNESSEE IS ONE of the most storied rivalries in college football, and it was always viewed by Coach Bryant as one of the most important games of the year. He was bitterly disappointed by the outcome of the 1965 game in Birmingham. With only a few seconds left in a game that was tied, 6-6, quarterback Kenny Stabler threw a pass out of bounds to kill the clock without realizing that it was fourth down. Bryant considered the incident to be the result of poor coaching and was determined to make up for the failure in the next encounter with the Volunteers.

It was evident that the coach was more fired up than usual as the team journeyed to Knoxville for the

1966 game. When the Crimson Tide arrived at the Knoxville airport, the team was met by a contingent from the local chamber of commerce. The orange-clad boosters handed out brochures that detailed local sight-seeing attractions to the players as they stepped off the plane.

"Fella, we didn't come up here for a damn tour of the Smoky Mountains. We came up here to play a damn football game."

When the president of the chamber of commerce handed a brochure and key chain to Coach Bryant, the coach took a quick glance and slammed the items to the floor. He told the man, "Fella, we didn't come up here for a damn tour of the Smoky Mountains. We came up here to play a damn football game."

27
The Lucky Bear

THE 1972 GAME WITH Tennessee in Knoxville was a classic in the third-Saturday-in-October series. Alabama was outplayed for most of the game and trailed, 10-3, with about four minutes left to play. At that point the Tide scored their first touchdown on a run by wishbone quarterback Terry Davis, cutting the Volunteers' lead to a single point. Many observers expected' Bama to attempt a two-point conversion to take the lead, but Coach Bryant surprised them by kicking the conversion to tie the score. His reasoning was that there was still plenty of time to stop the UT offense and get decent field position to set up a game-winning drive after a Volunteer punt.

His strategy was vindicated when Tennessee fumbled on the first play from scrimmage after the kickoff. The Crimson Tide recovered the Vol fumble at around the UT twenty-five-yard line, and a little while later quarterback Davis again scored on a run to give Alabama a 17-10 victory over its traditional rival.

As Coach Bryant left the stadium after the game and approached the team bus, he was confronted by an angry UT fan who got right in his face and yelled, "It could be you're a smart coach, but for sure you're the luckiest SOB in history." The Bear never broke stride as he tipped his trademark houndstooth hat and said, "Thank you."

28
Serious Football
on the Plains?

I N THE 1970s, DURING the week preceding the annual showdown with Auburn, Coach Bryant tried to call Auburn coach Shug Jordan at the Tigers' athletic department offices. The call was made at about 6:00 A.M. and after the phone went unanswered after several rings, the coach hung up.

At that point the Bear asked her, "Ma'am, don't you people at Auburn take your football seriously?"

After waiting a few minutes, Bryant again tried to call Jordan, but, still, nobody answered the phone. On the third attempt a member of the janitorial staff answered the phone, and the Bear told her who he was and that he wanted to speak with Coach Jordan. The lady explained that she was the only person in the building because the coaches did not arrive that early.

At that point the Bear asked her, "Ma'am, don't you people at Auburn take your football seriously?"

29
Houndstooth Power

ALABAMA ASSISTANT COACH Mal Moore and Coach Bryant were chauffeured by Billy Varner on a recruiting trip to Montgomery in the late 1970s. On the return trip to Tuscaloosa, an exhausted Coach Bryant was taking a nap in the backseat of the car when Varner unexpectedly slowed down. When the change in speed awakened the tired coach, Bryant asked the driver why he had slowed down. Varner replied that there was a highway patrolman right behind them, and he thought the officer was about to pull them over.

Coach Bryant took his trademark houndstooth hat and placed it in the back window of the car.

Upon hearing the driver's concern, Coach Bryant took his trademark houndstooth hat and placed it in the back window of the car. The power of the hat apparently worked since the trooper never did pull them over.

30
Woe Is Me

ALTHOUGH COLLEGE FOOTBALL coaches already had a long and distinguished tradition of understating the potential of their own team and overestimating their opponents' capabilities before Coach Bryant ever coached a game, he raised "poor mouthing" to an art form during his career. Former *Birmingham News* sports editor Clyde Bolton joined the *News* staff from the *Montgomery Advertiser* in the early 1960s without any previous sports-reporting experience.

The naive Bolton was soon assigned to cover Alabama football. The Crimson Tide's first opponent in 1961 was Georgia, and after Bolton had spent August listening to Coach Bryant's analysis of the strength of the two teams he told everyone he knew that the Tide had no chance of winning. Alabama's 32-6 thrashing of the Bulldogs convinced the rookie sportswriter that he would have to take the Bear's future prognostications with a grain of salt.

THE 1966 'BAMA TEAM seemed to be loaded with talent. The Tide had won the national championship in both 1964 and 1965, and it had a large number of returning starters from the 1965 team. However, during the 1966 preseason assessment of his team, Coach Bryant was "scared to death" because he only had one experienced quarterback on the team. His "fear" was not alleviated by the fact that the one quarterback happened to be All-American Kenny Stabler.

COACH BRYANT'S "POOR MOUTHING" was not confined solely to the press, however. Assistant coach Clem Gryska said that when the Bear gave the coaching staff his analysis of the upcoming opponent, it frequently appeared that the Tide would be a decided underdog. The head coach would tell the staff that several of the players on the upcoming opponent's roster were the best he had ever seen at their position. Frequently, the players that Coach Bryant bragged on were above-average performers, but he would never mention the opposing players that were *not* going to be serious competition to the Tide.

After the first six games of the 1978 season (in which Alabama would go on to win the national championship), Coach Bryant was not at all happy with his team or the coaching. The coach growled, "This is the poorest-coached team we've ever had. If I were the university administration, I'd be looking into the coaching staff."

31

"The Bear" Becomes "Coach Bryant"

IN THE EARLY 1970S ABC Sports sent a newly hired sportscaster to Tuscaloosa to do background work before a telecast of an Alabama football game. The announcer spent time with sports information director Kirk McNair while preparing for an interview with Coach Bryant. McNair was surprised to hear the young sportscaster continually refer to Coach Bryant as "Bear," and was curious as to whether his terminology would change during the actual interview with the coach.

When McNair and the announcer entered Coach Bryant's office, the sportscaster sat down on the coach's legendary couch. The couch was positioned right in front of Coach Bryant's desk, and its occupant sat even with the top of the coach's massive desk. At six feet four inches tall, Coach Bryant towered over the desk and the interviewer. As McNair expected, the reporter's terminology in addressing Coach Bryant in his office was different than it had been in the preliminary discussions they had had. The references to "Bear" were changed to Coach Bryant when the rookie announcer addressed the legendary coach. When the SID and the reporter left the coach's office at the conclusion of the interview, McNair said that the sportscaster "looked like a patient in a malaria ward" as the sweat poured off his brow.

32
Bear on the Links

C OACH BRYANT USED GOLF as a recreational outlet to escape the day-to-day rigors of coaching.
Although he enjoyed golf as an outlet, he was not
overly proficient on the links. He frequently played
with fellow Alabama graduate Charley Boswell, who
was one of the country's foremost blind golfers.

Boswell described the Bear's prowess on the
links by saying that he had never seen him play, "But
he's got the worst swing I've ever heard." Boswell
related a story where Bryant was playing a "normal
round—bad." The Coach blamed his bad round on
everything that he could think of—clubs, balls, the
weather, and, finally, the caddy. Bear finally told the
caddy that he was the worst in the entire world.

When the caddy protested his designation as the world's worst, Bear wanted to know why he disagreed with his assessment. The caddy answered that would be too much of a coincidence.

THE COACH HAD AN annual golf outing for members of the media in which he used the "Bryant modified" rules of golf. One of the features of these rules was that a player was allowed to move the ball one club length in any direction.

When Easterling later explained the incident to McNair, he explained that he had protested to Coach Bryant that his team should not take their ball out of the trap.

During one of the annual golf outings, former Alabama sports information director and Bryant confidante Kirk McNair noticed that one member of Coach Bryant's foursome had utilized the one-club-length rule to move the ball out of a sand trap by the green. *Huntsville Times* sports editor Bill Easterling was a member of this foursome, and McNair was surprised that Easterling, who was a stickler for the rules of golf, would allow this bending of the rules.

When Easterling later explained the incident to McNair, he explained that he had protested to Coach Bryant that his team should not take their ball out of the trap. When Bryant heard the sportswriter's complaint, he asked him, "Easterling, what's the name of this golf tournament?" When Easterling replied, "The Bear Bryant Golf Classic," Coach Bryant said, "That's right. Now take the ball out of the trap."

33
Police Escort

DURING FOOTBALL SEASON Coach Bryant had to be in Birmingham every Sunday morning at 9:00 A.M. to tape *The Bear Bryant Show*, which reviewed the prior day's game. He always tried to leave Tuscaloosa no later than eight o'clock to insure that he was in the studio on time. However, it was not unusual for him to be delayed at the athletic department in Tuscaloosa by autograph seekers and youngsters seeking to have their picture made with the legendary coach.

Assistant coach Clem Gryska related an instance in which they did not leave Tuscaloosa until 8:35 one Sunday morning. In order to make up some of the lost time, chauffeur Billy Varner put the pedal to the metal. When the driver passed a state trooper, the officer turned around in the median and gave chase to the tardy twosome. When Varner saw the patrolman turn around, he pulled over and waited for the officer to catch up with him. When the trooper approached the car with his ticket pad in hand, Varner told him of his predicament and asked if he could stop on the way back and clear up the paperwork associated with the speeding ticket.

When the officer saw Coach Bryant in the back seat, he told the driver to "follow me." He turned on the emergency lights and led them all the way to the television studio on Red Mountain in Birmingham. Of course, there was no longer a need for Varner to stop by the police station on the way back to do any paperwork.

34
Saint Bear

COACH BRYANT WAS remarkably successful after his return to his alma mater as he won three national championships in his first eight years at the Capstone. Some ardent Alabama fans began to ascribe divine powers to their ultra-successful coach.

Some ardent Alabama fans began to ascribe divine powers to their ultra-successful coach.

It was not uncommon to see automobile bumper stickers that showed the Bear walking on water over a script that said "We Believe." Golden Flake potato chips and Coca Cola sponsored his weekly television show, and an apocryphal story made the rounds in Alabama that Coach Bryant had fed a crowd of ten thousand Crimson Tide faithful with one Coca Cola and a bag of potato chips.

Assistant coach Clem Gryska related a story from the 1967 Sugar Bowl that gave further credence to the coach's supposed supernatural powers. That year's Sugar Bowl was played outdoors in the old Tulane Stadium. The Alabama team was much smaller and quicker than their opponents, the Nebraska Cornhuskers. Offensively, the Tide favored a wide-open passing attack that took advantage of the talents of All-American quarterback Kenny Stabler and a bevy of quick receivers, while Nebraska ran a straight-ahead ground game that utilized big running backs operating behind a massive offensive line.

Weather forecasters predicted cloudy and rainy conditions throughout the afternoon when the game was to be played. That type of weather would give Nebraska a big advantage since a muddy field would help the powerful Cornhusker running game and hamper the effectiveness of the Crimson Tide's high-powered aerial attack.

Alabama's chances didn't look good as rain fell throughout the morning of the game; but as soon as the Bear appeared on the field for the pregame workout the clouds parted and the sun came out. The sunshine continued throughout the game, and Alabama utilized its superior passing game to score twenty-four quick points and coast to a 34-7 victory over the Cornhuskers.

35
You Can Bet
on the Bear

I N THE MID-1960S Coach Bryant, businessman Red
Wells, Birmingham sportscaster Gary Sanders, and
Huntsville Times sports editor John Pruett were playing
golf at the coach's annual press outing. Bryant and
Pruett were tied with Wells and Sanders at the end of
eighteen holes, but Bryant was not satisfied with the
tie. The coach, who was credited with inventing the
phrase that "A tie is like kissing your sister," told
Wells that, "We ain't ending in no tie. We'll just play
these last three holes for fifty dollars a hole."

Pruett knew that fifty dollars a hole was chick-
en feed to Bryant and Wells, but he "probably didn't
have fifty dollars in his checking account, much less
on him." Pruett realized he was in a bind, and as he

recounted the story he asked, "What could I do? I couldn't say 'Well , Coach, I don't think I want to do that.' Not to Bear Bryant."

So Pruett had a private powwow with Sanders and told him to disregard their side of the fifty-dollar bet. As soon as Pruett and Sanders worked out their arrangement, Bryant birdied the first two holes to win the match for his team. The coach had not made a birdie all day, but he came through when the money was on the line. Pruett wanted to kick himself for not believing in the Bear as he contemplated his lost opportunity.

36
Bear, the Bard

NOVELIST JAMES A. MICHENER was an admirer of *Birmingham News* sports editor Alf Van Hoose and was amazed at the awe in which Van Hoose held Coach Bryant. Michener expressed a desire to meet the coaching "demigod" from Alabama, and the sportswriter arranged for a meeting of the famous novelist and the legendary coach.

Afterward, the novelist made it a point to spend some time with Coach Bryant whenever he had occasion to visit Alabama. After Bryant and John Underwood had published the Bryant autobiography, the legendary coach and the world-renowned author were both invited to attend the Alabama Sports Hall of Fame induction dinner in the late 1970s. Michener was doing research for his massive volume entitled *Sports in America*, and he accepted Van Hoose's invitation to the banquet because he was assured by the sportswriter that he would get a chance to interview Bryant again.

As Van Hoose introduced the coach to the author he said, "Coach, you remember Jim Michener, don't you?" Bear responded with "Oh, yeah, yeah." At that point the author paid Bryant a compliment by saying, "Coach, you don't know what it does to an author's ego to come into a town with a book (*Centennial*) and find that another author is outselling him three to one." Bear laughed at Michener's comment, and they chatted a few more minutes before a local television station pulled the author away for an interview.

When Michener departed, Van Hoose explained to the coach that the novelist had paid him a great compliment because Michener's books had outsold any books ever published except the Bible.

When Michener departed, Van Hoose explained to the coach that the novelist had paid him a great compliment because Michener's books had outsold any books ever published except the Bible. He named the novelist's big bestsellers to

Coach Bryant and observed, "That was a pretty good compliment he paid you." The Bear digested the comment for a minute and then said, "Hell, it ought to have been fifteen to one."

37

West Alabama Meets the Lower East Side

COACH BRYANT'S DICTION could be hard for native Southerners to understand and downright unintelligible for folks from north of the Mason-Dixon line. In the late 1970s, as Bryant approached Amos Alonzo Stagg's record for most career victories by a college football coach, *Playboy* magazine decided that it was time to do a major story on the legendary coach. The magazine dispatched Richard Price, a well-known writer of movies and novels, to the sunny south to chronicle Alabama's most famous resident.

Although Price had impeccable literary credentials, his street-smart New York City background put him at a distinct disadvantage in

understanding the Bear's southern drawl. As Price
interviewed Bryant in his Tuscaloosa office, he
posed a question to the coach regarding motivation. The coach modestly allowed that he had
never found any secret motivational techniques,
and even if he had he would be reluctant to tell
anyone what they were. As the coach
continued on the subject of motivation,
he delivered a five-minute discourse, of
which the puzzled New Yorker understood
very little. Bryant ended his commentary
with a hearty laugh and remarked that
apparently his joke had not been funny to
his interviewer. The embarrassed New
Yorker protested that he had indeed
found the joke to be funny and let out a
belated attempt at a laugh.

*The coach
ended his
commen-
tary with a
hearty
laugh and
remarked
that appar-
ently his
joke had
not been
funny to
his inter-
viewer.*

Later, as Price was wrapping up loose
ends on his story before returning to New
York, he scheduled a meeting with Kirk
McNair, Alabama's sports information director.
The writer opened the session by telling McNair
and a couple of his colleagues in the athletic
department about the joke and complaining, "I
didn't understand a damn thing he said." When
Price played back his tape recording of Bryant's

joke-anecdote for the group in McNair's office, he expected the southerners to sympathize with him about the old coach's diction. Instead of the expected commiseration, the Alabamians were soon all on the floor howling at Bryant's joke. The assistant trainer remarked that he had never heard that one before as he wiped tears of laughter from his eyes. McNair cackled that it was "the funniest thing I ever heard."

At that point, McNair "translated" the joke for the Yankee writer. He began by explaining that the Bear was recalling an old Kentucky-Tennessee game from his days as the mentor of the Wildcats. During the halftime break, a spell-binding orator named Doc Rhodes went into the Kentucky locker room and delivered what Bryant described as the "damnedest talk I ever heard." Rhodes's pep talk had a huge lineman so fired up that the Bear said he was "slobbering at the bit." The only problem was that the hyper lineman was not even playing. When a fourth-quarter Tennessee drive reached Kentucky's fifteen-yard line, Bryant decided it was time to send his highly motivated lineman into the

During the halftime break, a spell-binding orator named Doc Rhodes went into the Kentucky locker room and delivered what Bryant described as the "damnedest talk I ever heard."

107

fray. When the player was finally sent into the game, he charged halfway onto the field and then retreated to the sidelines where he said, "Coach, can Doc Rhodes talk at me again?"

38

Is It Live or Is It Memorex?

S UNDAY AFTERNOON AT four o'clock during football season was the time that all Alabama football fans could be found huddled around their TV sets watching *The Bear Bryant Show*, which was produced live every week from a Birmingham television studio. Of course, all of the assistant coaches and athletic department employees were at work at their offices in the athletic department when the show came on, but they would take a break from their Sunday chores to watch the boss on TV. Since the best TV in the athletic department was in Coach Bryant's office, most of the athletic department staffers would watch the show from there.

Assistant coaches Mal Moore and Dude Hennessey both did great impersonations of Coach

Laughing with the Bear

Bryant's gruff voice, and one of them would normally pretend to be Coach Bryant coming into his office during the show. One Sunday as the entourage watched the coach's TV performance, Hennessey was sitting in Coach Bryant's chair with his feet propped up on his desk. As the gathering intently watched the show, little attention was paid to Coach Bryant's voice saying, "Dude, do you mind if I have my chair?" Hennessey replied, "You can have it when I'm finished with it." However, when Dude turned around he was surprised to see that the voice was not coming from Mal Moore but from Coach Bryant himself. The TV station had switched from a live performance to videotape, and the coach's unexpected appearance touched off a mad scramble in his office.

39
Potpourri

ANY TIME THERE were complaints about football tickets, Coach Bryant said that the "Ticket Committee" handled ticket issues. Former Alabama sports information director Kirk McNair said that he had never heard of such a committee and did not know of anyone who was on the committee. Apparently the "committee" was a device that Coach Bryant used to shield himself from unhappy ticket purchasers.

After a ragged practice session in the spring of 1973, Coach Bryant remarked to McNair, "We looked like a cow college out there today." The Tide had lost to Auburn the previous year and one of the reasons given for Alabama's loss was that Coach

Bryant had been quoted as calling Auburn "a cow college" before the 1972 game. As he pondered how his remark to McNair would look in print as he puffed on a Chesterfield, he told the SID to "change that to a barber college."

Lineman Charley Pell promptly drew blood by slamming his helmet against the side of his head, and at that Coach Bryant proceeded to declare the practice session over.

ALABAMA'S PRACTICE SESSIONS during the Bryant era were known to be extremely physical. Long-time 'Bama trainer Jim Gostree said that if he wrote a book about his tenure with Coach Bryant it would be called "You Can't Make an Omelet without Breaking a Few Eggs."

In the early 1960s Coach Bryant was disappointed that a practice session had not been "physical" enough to suit him, and he told the players that practice would not end until he saw some blood. Upon hearing this, lineman Charley Pell promptly drew blood by slamming his helmet against the side of his head, and at that Coach Bryant proceeded to declare the practice session over.

COACH BRYANT SURROUNDED himself with bright assistant coaches, and he had an unusually large number of assistants who went on to head-coaching jobs at other schools and in professional football. Former Georgia coach Vince Dooley once remarked, "Coach Bryant has put a lot of people into coaching. But he's put a lot of them out of coaching, too."

ONE NIGHT COACH BRYANT was faring poorly while playing gin at the Indian Hills Country Club in Tuscaloosa. After he had lost all of the cash he had brought with him, he wrote an IOU. One of the other participants in the card game had had previous experience with Bryant IOU's and promptly told the coach that it was a cash game and IOU's were not allowed. Coach Bryant told the protester, "I've got more money than you'll ever think about having. That IOU is good." The other card player then told the coach, "I'm not worried about your money. I'm worried about your memory."

40
Yes, Dear

Although sportswriters always relished the chance for a one-on-one interview with Coach Bryant, they were frequently frustrated in their efforts to get through the interview session without multiple interruptions. Frequent disturbances by incoming phone calls were the norm. *Huntsville Times* sports editor John Pruett described an especially frustrating interview with the Bear where it seemed that every time he and the coach would begin talking, the phone would ring. The caller was invariably another coach who was calling to get the Bear's opinion of his upcoming opponent.

On most occasions Bryant would talk to the caller for ten minutes or so. On about the fifth incoming call, Bryant answered the phone and told the caller to wait a minute while he looked for a pencil with which to write. After finding his writing instrument, he said, "All right, go ahead. A carton of milk, a loaf of bread, a can of tuna." After the gruff old coach hung up, he said, "Damn, you'd think Mary Harmon (his wife) could go shopping for groceries."

Bibliography

Axthelm, Pete, "The Mastery of the Bear," *Newsweek*. February 7, 1983.

Browning, Al , "Dawn of a New Era," article in Paul W. Bryant Museum.

————, *I Remember Paul "Bear" Bryant,* Nashville: Cumberland House Publishing, 2001.

Bryant, Paul and John Underwood, *Bear: The Hard Life and Good Times of Alabama's Coach Bryant.* Boston and Toronto: Little, Brown, and Company, 1972.

Coach Hank Crisp Stories—Remembered by Hank's Boys, 1979. Paul W. Bryant Museum.

Deford, Frank, " I Do Love the Football," *Sports Illustrated*. November 13, 1981.

Dent, Jim, *The Junction Boys: How Ten Days in Hell with Bear Bryant Forged a Champion.* New York: St. Martin's, 1999.

Dunnavant, Keith, *Coach—The Life of Paul "Bear" Bryant.* New York: Simon and Schuster, 1996.

Frady, Marshall, "The Bear in Winter," *Sport.* September 1975.

Freeman, Don, *San Diego Union*, April 1990.

Laughing with the Bear

Herskowitz, Mickey, *The Legend of Bear Bryant*, New York: McGraw-Hill, 1987.

Kastelz, Bill, *Florida Times-Union*, October 17, 1978.

Michener, James A, *Sports in America*, New York: Random House, 1976.

Lumpkin, Bill, "Bear." *Birmingham Post-Herald*, November 29 , 1981.

Oates, Bob, "The Year of the Bear." *Los Angeles Times*, September 9, 1981.

Price, Richard, "Bear Bryant's Miracles," *Playboy*. October 1979.

Pruett, John, *Huntsville Times*, December 20, 2002; January 22, 2003.

Reed, Delbert, *Paul "Bear" Bryant—What Made Him a Winner*. Tuscaloosa: VisionPress, 1995.

"The Legend," *The Sporting News*, November 15, 1980.

Van Hoose, Alf, "Bear Remembered," 1983 Alabama football program.

―――, "Memories of a Great Coach," article in Paul W. Bryant Museum.

West, Marvin, article in Paul W. Bryant Museum.

Notes

The following sources were used:

1. **The Young Cub.** "The Legend," *The Sporting News*. Alf Van Hoose, " Memories of a Great Coach." Don Freeman, *San Diego Union*. Alf Van Hoose, "Bear Remembered."

2. **The Bear in Love.** Bryant and Underwood, *Bear: The Hard Life and Good Times of Alabama's Coach Bryant*, p. 36. Al Browning, "Dawn of a New Era."

3. **So You Want to Quit?** *Coach Hank Crisp Stories—Remembered by Hank's Boys.*

4. **The One-Legged Terror in Knoxville.** Delbert Reed, *Paul "Bear" Bryant—What Made Him a Winner*, pp. 26–27 . Mickey Herskowitz, *The Legend of Bear Bryant*, p. 45. Bryant and Underwood, pp. 48–49. Kirk McNair speech to Eufaula Touchdown Club.

5. **Give the Boy Some Coffee.** Reed, p. 135. Bryant and Underwood, p. 93. Bill Lumpkin, "Bear."

6. **Heavenly Recruiting.** Bryant and Underwood, pp. 73–74. *Keith Dunnavant, Coach—The Life of Paul "Bear" Bryant*, pp. 76–77. Bob Oates, "The Year of the Bear."

7. **The Bear and the Baron.** Herskowitz, p. 72. Bryant and Underwood, pp. 118–121. Clem Gryska interview.

8. **The Professors "Investigate" the Baron.** Herskowitz, p. 72. Bryant and Underwood, pp. 119–120.

9. **Home for the Holidays.** Reed, p. 123. Herskowitz, pp. 60–61. Dunnavant, pp. 72–73. Al Browning, *I Remember Paul "Bear" Bryant*, p. 89. Jim Dent, *The Junction Boys: How Ten Days in Hell with Bear Bryant Forged a Champion*, p. 153.

10. **Good for the Goose and the Gander.** Reed, p. 139. Bryant and Underwood, pp. 189–190.

Laughing with the Bear

11. **Sleeping in Church.** Herskowitz, p. 239. Dent, pp. 134–138. Dennis Goehring interview.

12. **You Can't Run Me Off.** Herskowitz, p. 33. Bryant and Underwood, p. 135. Dunnavant, pp. 101–111. Dent, pp. 65-66. Goehring interview.

13. **Recruiting Aggies.** Bryant and Underwood, pp. 129–138. Dent, p. 11.

14. **The Mustard Seed.** Bryant and Underwood, pp. 6–7. Dent, pp. 175–183. Goehring interview.

15. **Poor Henry.** Herskowitz, pp. 95–96. Dent, pp. 212–213. Goehring interview.

16. **Running for His Life.** Herskowitz, pp. 109-110. Bryant and Underwood, pp. 149–150. Dunnavant, p. 126. Browning, p. 143.

17. **The Chiefs and the Indians.** Reed, p. 119. Bryant and Underwood, pp. 138, 323. Frank Deford, "I Do Love the Football." Gryska interview.

18. **Help from the Domino Club.** Dunnavant, p. 137. Gryska interview.

19. **You Need a New Car.** Browning, pp. 172–173. Gryska interview.

20. **Who Hired that Idiot?** Bryant and Underwood, pp. 167–168. Baxter Booth interview. Gryska interview.

21. **Hold that Line—Or Else.** Booth interview. *Huntsville Times*, November 16, 1958.

22. **Firing the Quarterback.** Reed, pp. 103–105. Bryant and Underwood, pp. 172–174. Dunnavant, pp. 146–148. Gryska interview.

23. **The Pygmy and the Giant.** Alf Van Hoose, "Memories of a Great Coach." Bob Oates, "The Year of the Bear." Marshall Frady, "The Bear in Winter." Gryska interview.

Notes

24. **No Springs—Honest Weight.** Herskowitz, pp. 160–161. Bryant and Underwood, p. 267. McNair interview.

25. **Helping the Hoopsters.** "The Legend," *The Sporting News*. McNair interview.

26. **Welcome to Knoxville**. Browning, pp. 115–116. Gryska interview.

27. **The Lucky Bear.** Browning, p. 152. Marvin West article in Bryant Museum.

28. **Serious Football on the Plains**. Bryant and Underwood, p. 7. Browning, pp. 125–126.

29. **Houndstooth Power.** John Pruett, *Huntsville Times*.

30. **Woe Is Me.** Bill Kastelz, *Florida Times-Union*. John Pruett, *Huntsville Times*. McNair interview. Gryska interview.

31. **"The Bear" Becomes "Coach Bryant."** McNair interview.

32. **Bear on the Links.** Alf Van Hoose, "Bear Remembered." McNair speech to Eufaula Quarterback Club.

33. **Police Escort.** Gryska interview.

34. **Saint Bear.** Browning, pp. 256–257. Pete Axthelm, "The Mastery of the Bear." Gryska interview.

35. **You Can Bet on the Bear.** John Pruett, *Huntsville Times*.

36. **Bear, the Bard.** Herskowitz, pp. 240–241. James A. Michener, *Sports in America*, pp. 220, 230, 333. McNair interview.

37. **West Alabama Meets the Lower East Side.** Richard Price, "Bear Bryant's Miracles." McNair interview.

38. **Is It Live or Is It Memorex?** McNair speech to the Eufaula Quarterback Club.

39. **Potpourri.** McNair speech to Eufaula Quarterback Club.

40. **Yes, Dear.** John Pruett, *Huntsville Times*.

Author

Author Richard Sikes, a resident of Madison, Alabama, is a manufacturing financial executive and part-time historian who loves swapping stories with the best of them. He is a life-long fan of Coach Bryant and the Alabama Crimson Tide. This is his first book.